IKEBANA

Season to Season

IKEBANA
Season to Season

Noriko Ohno
KOKUSAI IKEBANA ASSOCIATION

KODANSHA INTERNATIONAL
Tokyo • New York • London

Distributed in the United States by Kodansha America, Inc., 114
Fifth Avenue, New York, New York 10011, and in the United
Kingdom and continental Europe by Kodansha Europe Ltd., 95
Aldwych, London WC2B 4JF. Published by Kodansha
International Ltd., 17-14 Otowa 1-chome, Bunkyo-ku, Tokyo 112,
and Kodansha America, Inc. Copyright © 1995 by Kodansha
International Ltd. All rights reserved. Printed in Japan.

ISBN 4-7700-2020-1
First edition, 1995
95 96 97 7 6 5 4 3 2 1

CONTENTS

FOREWORD

People everywhere love beautiful flowers and arrange them for all kinds of occasions in their daily lives. Like poems, flower arrangements can be formal or informal, happy or sad, spontaneous or serious. It is simply a part of human nature to celebrate special events or to express emotions by using flowers.

The word *ikebana* itself is formed from *ikiru* ("to keep alive") and *hana* ("flowers"), and the art of flower arrangement had its origins in this natural principle. However, over the centuries the various styles of ikebana developed into rival schools, which made the art inaccessible to all but the most committed students. As ikebana slowly traveled overseas, it was presented as a codified art form, full of rigid, intimidating rules.

In 1955, I established the Kokusai ("International") Ikebana Association in the hope of dispelling that severe image and opening up ikebana to everyone who loves flowers. I was also convinced that fresh input from abroad would revitalize ikebana, propelling it outside the bounds of each school and into a global art form that respects individuality and embraces modernity. In this way, ikebana would be both an element of and an active participant in international cultural communication.

Since then, my belief that ikebana itself is international, and not confined to any particular method, continues to deepen through the many international friendships I have developed. Though ornamental Western floral art uses blossoms as design material only, the Japanese attitude toward floral arrangement is much deeper and more spiritual. The two most important philosophies of ikebana—that the arrangement fits the environment in which it is displayed, and that the emotions and character of the person are expressed in the arrangement—are precisely what makes ikebana, in its ideal state, adaptable to so many countries, to so many flowers, and especially to so many people.

The constant interaction between Japanese and non-Japanese arrangers has resulted in a free form of ikebana incorporating the colors, flowers, and containers of many countries. In the back of this book I have included basic directions presenting the standard styles and techniques taught in ikebana, but from my own creations you will see that I encourage all sorts of variations—even humorous ones. I have chosen plain backgrounds to emphasize the flowers and containers, but I hope your arrangements will also involve space, music, and other design elements. I have included an example of the Morimono style, using *Cymbidium goeringi*, with the roots carefully washed and blossoms placed among them. This is a traditional ikebana style, but I have given it a modern touch. Such arrangements were intended for the *tokonoma*, but with flowers such as roses or fruits, they are ideal as centerpieces on tables.

I have dedicated one section to my travels in Latin America. Wherever I travel, I try to respect the traditions and history of the various countries and incorporate these into my creations. In other words, I try to blend this Japanese art with the culture of each country.

I hope you will enjoy this book and use it whenever you need hints for your own arrangements.

THE HISTORY OF IKEBANA

The history of ikebana is long indeed, and its origins date to Buddhist ritual flower offerings (*kuge*) of the sixth and seventh centuries, when Buddhism was first transmitted to Japan. The famous eleventh-century miscellany "Makura no Soshi" (*The Pillow Book*) mentions "Cherry blossoms in a celadon vase," and diaries of the Kamakura period (1185–1333) speak of flowers arranged for Tanabata, the Festival of the Stars that takes place in July.

Formal ikebana, however, is traditionally said to date from the Muromachi period (1392–1568). This was an age of widespread rivalry among the feudal lords, and the ensuing wars led to the destruction of Kyoto, the seat of culture. But it was also an age when lively and exciting new art forms evolved. Ikebana, one of these new developments, ceased being a way of arranging floral offerings to the Buddha and began to crystallize as an art form appreciated in itself. *Tatebana* ("standing flowers") became a fashionable and elaborate flower arrangement style—better known by the name *rikka*—that shared pride of place with a special brand of floral arrangement simultaneously developed at the Imperial Court.

At that time, the townspeople were rapidly becoming more

prosperous and were putting on floral shows that rivaled those of the court nobles. These exhibitions gradually developed into formal associations, the forebears of the now-famous ikebana schools. As ikebana grew into a full-fledged art, there was a noticeable shift in attention from the flowers to the arrangers. Then, just when the *rikka* style became even more elaborate, the tea ceremony came into fashion. The flowery *rikka* floral arrangements were found to be completely unsuited for the Zen-inspired tea ceremonies and another style was sorely needed. This was invented by the tea masters themselves: the charming and simple *nageire* (literally "tossed in") style, also known as *chabana*, or "tea flowers."

Nageire is characterized by the aesthetic of a single blossom and a single leaf. The aim of this simplicity was to reproduce the appearance of flowers growing in their natural setting. As the refined tastes of the tea ceremony gained in popularity, so too did the *nageire* style, which soon demanded simple, rough vases with subtle colors to replace the painted porcelain ones that were previously in vogue. Baskets made of bamboo and fitted with containers for water made superb tea-ceremony flower containers, as we can tell from the famous flower basket now in Onjo-ji temple and attributed to the most famous tea master of all, Sen no Rikyu.

Gradually, over the centuries, ikebana developed into an ornamental and artistic form so deeply infused with the Japanese love of beauty and nature that flower arranging has become not just an art form but more a philosophy and an aesthetic that is much treasured by all Japanese people.

IKEBANA
Season to Season

The New Year

Theme: Spring Celebration
Materials: Camellia, *Cymbidium goeringi*
Container: Stand of Wajima lacquer

In Japan, red and white are the traditional colors associated with celebration. In this Morimono-style arrangement, the roots of the *Cymbidium goeringi* are spread out as if to disperse the feeling of festivity conveyed by the camellias and the turtle.

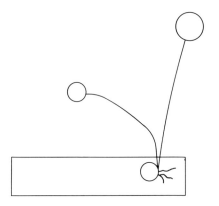

Theme: Happy New Year
Materials: Bird of Paradise, Bird of Paradise leaf, Willow
Container: White vase

Placed upright as a backdrop, the bird of paradise leaf accentuates the graceful flowing lines of the willow. The bird seems posed for flight, calling out "Happy New Year!"

Notes: This vase can be placed in different positions for other creations. Wipe the Bird of Paradise leaf with an unscented oil to bring out its natural gloss and color.

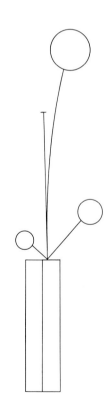

Theme: Joy at the New Year
Materials: Pine, Anthurium, Willow
Container: Shallow vase acquired in Luxembourg

The red container and the white anthurium express the
joyful sentiments associated with welcoming the New Year.
The bold pine and elegant willow add a rhythmic tone to
the arrangement. Pine and willow are customary in New
Year arrangements: the pine represents longevity, and the
willow knot symbolizes the ties that link people together.

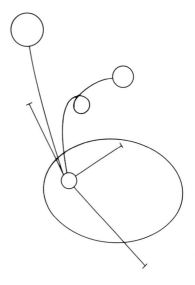

Theme: New Year Greetings
Materials: Narcissus, Nandina
Container: White vase

Pert narcissuses with red Nandina berries at their base pro-
vide a delightful foretaste of spring. The carefree grace of
the narcissuses is reinforced by the varying lengths of the
flower stems and the vivid color of the berries.

Note: Nandina berries play an important role in New Year celebrations since they are believed to usher in good fortune and to
change bad luck to good.

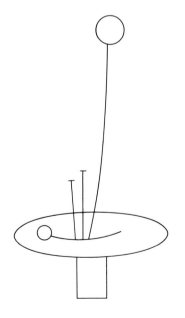

Spring

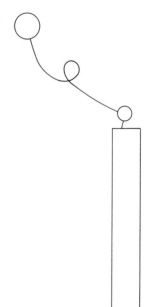

Theme: Smiles
Materials: Camellia, Bear Grass
Container: Blue vase

The beautiful mix of red and white in the single camellia bloom evokes the smile of an innocent young girl, and the bear grass creates a delicate silhouette in the arrangement.

Note: Wipe the camellia leaves with a soft cloth to bring out their natural gloss and color. Use a generous amount of bear grass to make the knot.

Theme: A Breath of Spring

Materials: Pink Rose, Flowering Fern

Container: Black ceramic vases speckled with gold
  dust (designed by the author)

The fern fronds seem to be swaying gently in the warm
spring breeze, whose sweet fragrance is embodied in the
pink roses.

Note: The expressiveness of the composition can be further
enhanced by subtly positioning the three matching vases.

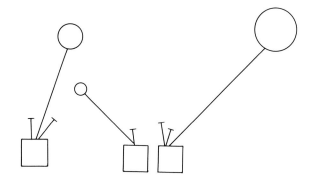

Theme: Encounter with a Tile
Materials: Camellia
Container: Tile stand

The camellias are carefully arranged on a large flat plate that resembles a tile (*kawara*). The blossoms seem to look out expectantly, as though seeking someone to chat to.

Note: The tip of the camellia stem should be wrapped in pre-soaked gauze, covered with foil, and hidden under the stone. This method will allow you to enjoy the flower much longer.

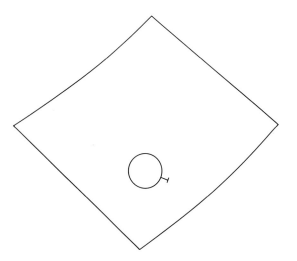

Theme: Spring Waltz
Materials: Spirea, Tulip, dried leaves
Container: Vase from Estonia

The sweet and innocent colors of spirea and tulips are totally in harmony, dancing a floral waltz to the music of spring. The rhythm is set by the dried leaves.

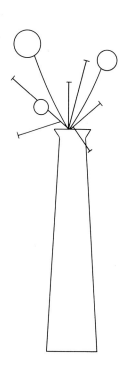

Theme: Beautiful Spring (Elegant Lines)
Materials: Mulberry, Wattle
Container: White ceramic pigeon ornament (made in
    Italy)

The pigeons appear to be enjoying themselves, pecking at
the yellow wattle, while the mulberry sways in the breeze,
showing off its elegant lines.

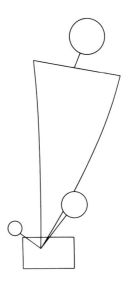

Theme: Tulips on Clouds
Materials: Tulips, nylon net (acquired in Denmark)
Container: Dark blue vase

Looking up at the sky and daydreaming, I suddenly had a vision of tulips peeking out from behind the clouds, proclaiming the arrival of spring.

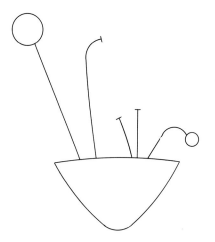

Theme: Awakening of Spring
Materials: Golden Bells, Tulip, Iris leaf
Container: Silver vase (made in Brazil)

Beauty lies in the perfect harmony between the flowers
themselves, the vase, and the surroundings of the arrangement. Here, the red tulip and the silver vase make a daz-
zling combination, whose beauty is enhanced by the
golden bells and the handsome lines of the iris leaves. The
whole presents a dramatic announcement of spring's awakening.

Note: Spring flowers are extremely delicate and need a lot of
water, so the *mizukiri* technique should be used.

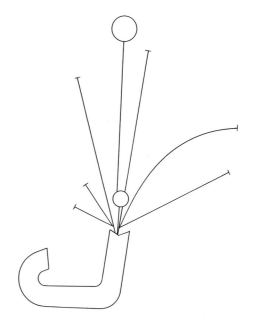

Theme: Spring in Full Bloom
Materials: Calla, Rose, Sweet Pea, Statice
Container: White vase

The calla trills a joyous song of spring, backed by a floral
chorus of vibrant red, pink, and purple.

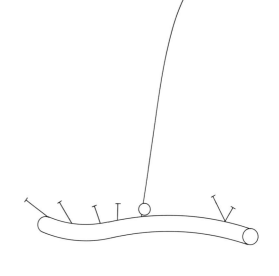

Theme: Sounds of Spring
Materials: Barley, Calla
Container: Glass vase and shallow red glass vase

The vivid contrast between the red vase and the white calla
makes a bold statement of the coming of spring, with the
season's soft footsteps echoed in the crystal balls. The barley, one of spring's star performers, highlights this effect.

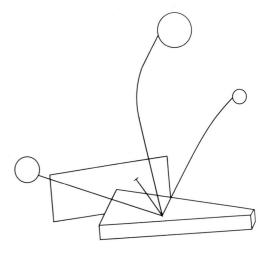

Summer

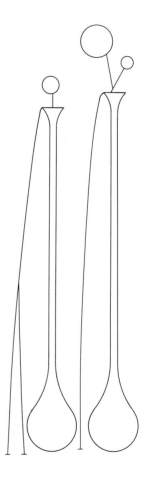

Theme: Whirling Flower Petals
Materials: Clematis, Fennel, Asparagoides
Container: Glass vases

The petals of the flowers here join in a lively dance, whirling in the breeze.

Note: Spray water on the leaves to make them look fresh. When cutting the flower stems, the *mizukiri* technique should be used.

Theme: Summer Poetry

Materials: Allium, Giganteum, Spathe flowers, Bird
of Paradise leaf, glass flowers, glass tube

Container: Glass vase

The exquisite lines of the flowers recite summery verses
while the glass flowers and rod add a cool, refreshing touch
amid the heat of summer.

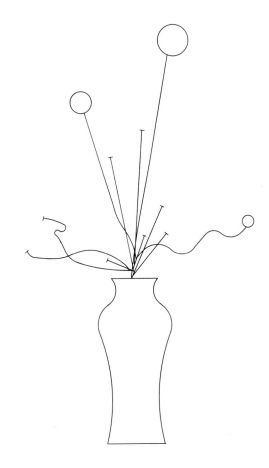

Theme: News of Summer
Materials: Wild Grape, Sunflower
Container: Three yellow vases

The sunflower makes a loud and unequivocal declaration
of summer.

Note: The sunflower is a common symbol of summer both in
Japan and in many other countries.

Theme: Floating Flower
Materials: Sunflower, Lemon
Container: Glass vase

The sunflower enjoys a respite from the heat, refreshed by the scent of the lemon and the soothing coolness of the water.

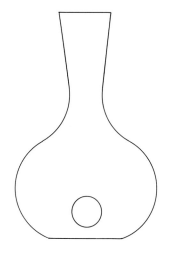

Theme: Lifelong Devotion to Flowers
Materials: Allium, Spathe flower, Bird of Paradise leaf
Container: Two glass vases of different shades of
    green, one placed inside the other

This might be regarded as a self-portrait. The allium symbolizes my life with flowers, while the spathe flower,
standing very straight and upright in the vase, expresses my
wholehearted devotion to flowers.

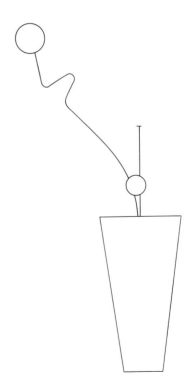

Theme: Water Arrangement
Materials: Water, Water Lilies, crystal balls
Container: White glassware (made in Finland)

The water deftly sets afloat the two water lilies and the leaf, while soothing them amid the hot summer air. The crystal balls lend the water an icy chill, and the contrast between the water and the white vases evokes a natural coolness. The arrangement of the water lilies was inspired by the ladies in the Renoir painting.

Note: Very clear and clean water should be used.

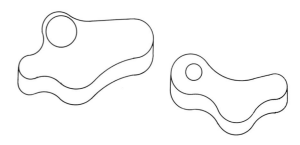

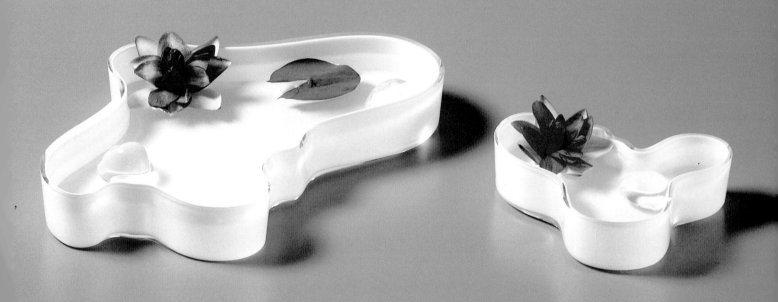

Theme: Flowers of June
Materials: Japanese Bulrush, Calla, Carnation, Asplenium
Container: Baccarat vase

The name of the white lily—calla—means "beautiful" in Greek. I arranged the calla in a French Baccarat vase to express my good wishes and hopes of happiness for the newly wedded Crown Prince and Princess of Japan. These fresh, fragrant flowers were picked in a village called Koyasu, which is near Hayama in Kanagawa Prefecture.

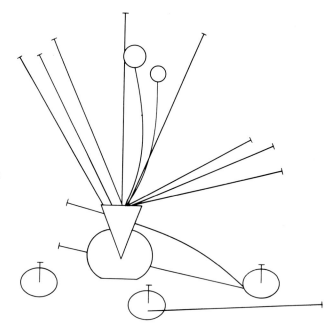

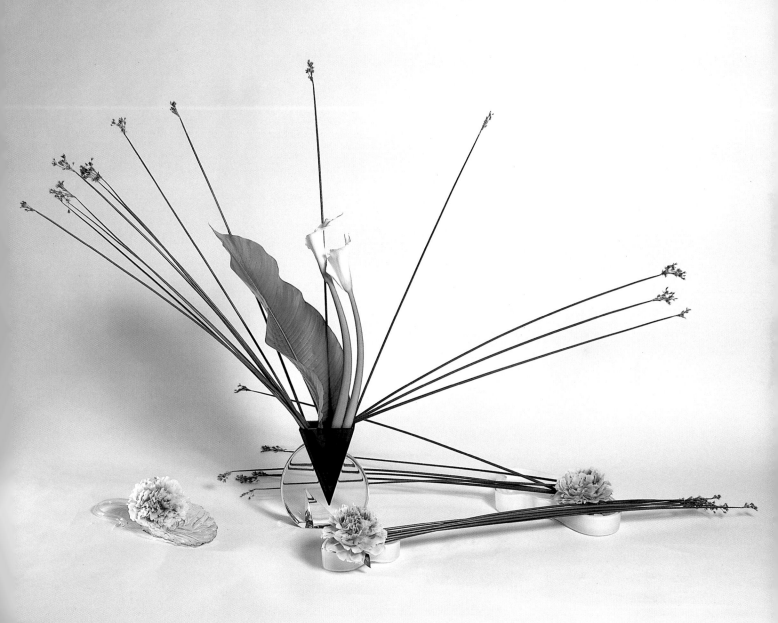

Theme: A Distant Dream
Materials: Japanese Bulrush, East Indian Lotus flower
    and leaf, Themeda Triandra
Container: Loosely woven basket with bamboo vase

The themeda triandra gently salutes the lotus, while the
leaf and the bulrush sway dreamily, stirred by an occasional
breath of wind.

Note: The basket can be placed in different positions to vary the
creation and its effect.

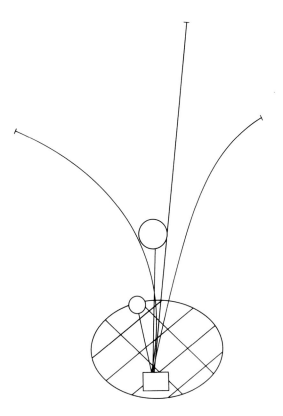

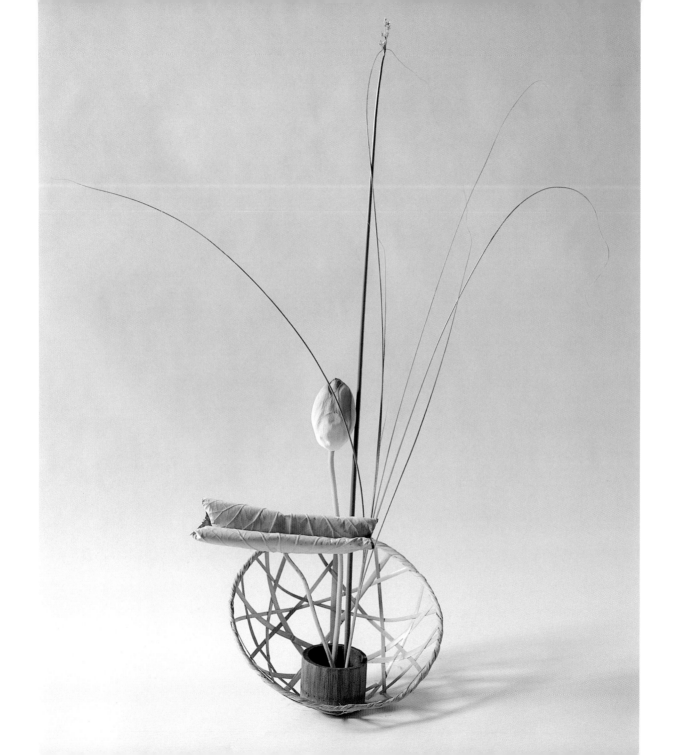

Autumn

Theme: Whirling Flower Petals

Materials: Chinese Mahonia, Oncidium, Japanese
  Bittersweet, Lycoris

Container: Vase made in England

The excitement of a spectacular Autumn Ball is heightened by the elegant dance of the yellow oncidium and
other vivacious guests.

Note: Autumn flowers, especially the stems, are very delicate and
need to be handled with special care. Use the *mizukiri* technique,
and dip in alcohol to prevent the growth of bacteria. The color
combination of the flowers is of the utmost importance.

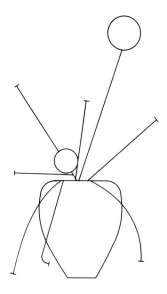

Theme: Poetic Autumn
Materials: Bamboo Reed, Corn
Container: Yellow vase designed by the author

As we sit back and relax, the strains of delightful Autumn poems chanted in perfect harmony come to our ears.

Note: Use the *mizukiri* technique for both the bamboo reed and the corn, and dip the tip of the bamboo reed in wine or saké. Take care not to bend the reed since its beauty lies in its splendid, upright stem.

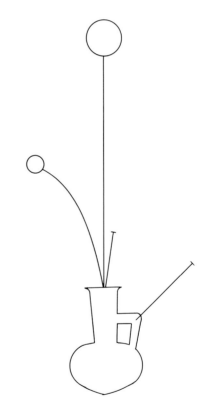

Theme: The Soul of Flowers

Materials: Rose, Lemon, Asparagus, Japanese Plume Grass

Container: Red glass vase, a souvenir from Spain.

The lemon and the rose represent the essence of flowers with radiant autumn colors.

Countless words of praise are lavished on flowers, but each flower has only one soul, and to attain that soul, we must all strive along our individual paths. No matter how many days or years have passed, we must continue as if this is our first step today.—Noriko Ohno

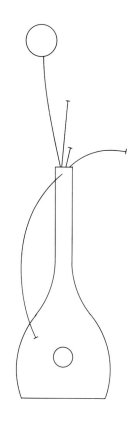

Theme: Invitation to Baccarat

Materials: Smoke Tree, Sweet Pea, Kangaroo Paw, Amaryllis, Bishop's Weed, heads of Japanese Plume Grass

Container: Baccarat vases

This cheerful composition is a combination of two arrangements (combination style). The mesmerizing contrast created by pink amaryllis blossoms and blue Baccarat vases is accentuated by the rare kangaroo paw.

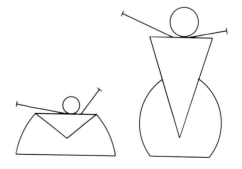

Theme: Autumn Poem
Materials: Gompho Carpus, Japanese Bittersweet,
  Japanese Rowan, Japanese Plume Grass
Container: Antique Japanese vase

The vibrant colors evoke a powerful impression of autumn.
The red buds of the Japanese bittersweet pop open as if to
orchestrate this chorus of autumn harmonies.

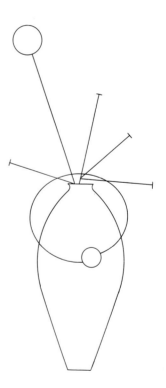

Theme: A Whisper

Materials: Japanese Chestnut, Chinese Catalpa, *Kashiwa-gomu*

Container: Vase from Southern France

The exquisite counterpoint of the Chinese catalpa and the *kashiwagomu* creates a serene, hushed mood, with Japanese chestnut peeking out as if to whisper something.

Note: Take care not to bend or alter the shape of the Chinese catalpa, but let it hang naturally.

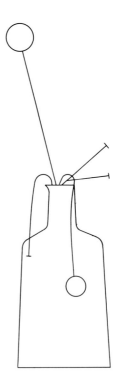

Theme: Above a Cloud
Materials: Corn Flag (Gladiolus), Whispering Willow
Container: Two vases, placed one on top of the other

The willow is arranged in a circular shape and resembles a fluffy cloud drifting lazily across the sky. Above it the pink gladiolus shines out like a vision of romance. Placing the vases this way is a new technique that adds character to the arrangement.

Note: When bending the willows, care should be taken to avoid breaking any twigs.

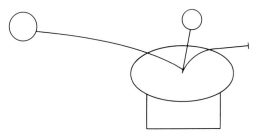

Theme: The Universe of Flowers
Materials: Cockscomb, Aspidistra, Blackberries
Container: Oval vase and ceramic ornament

The view through the circular ornament affords a glimpse
of the wonderful realm of flowers.

Note: Exciting arrangements can be achieved by judiciously
changing the placement of the vase and ornament.

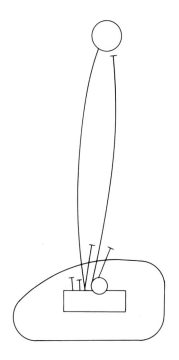

Theme: On Wings of Beauty
Materials: Stony Willow, Caladium, Arand Christine
Container: Vase with two mouths

The stately stony willow sprays convey an impression of
the strength and reliability of the wings of an airplane.

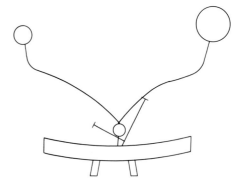

Theme: Colors of Autumn
Materials: Lily, Autumn leaves
Container: Bizen vase

By using complementary colors and materials found only
in autumn you can reinforce the impact of that season's
atmosphere. With the blaze of autumn colors comes a
serene and mature fulfillment. I hope each one of you will
be able to feel your own autumn.

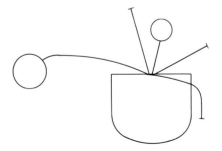

Winter

Theme: Winter Story
Materials: Willow, White Camellia, black metal rose
Container: White ceramic vase

The willow is entwined around part of the vase to create rhythm and movement. The white camellia softens the wintry feeling of cold sharpness emanating from the black rose.

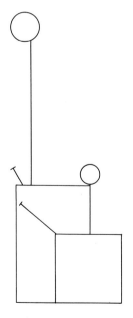

Theme: Flower Diary
Materials: Monstera, Anthurium, Bear Grass
Container: White vase placed inside a black vase

Keeping a daily diary with flowers is the most satisfying
and fulfilling activity that I know.

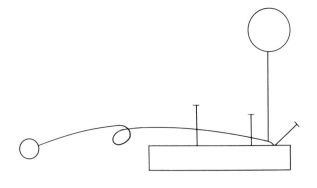

Theme: Flames
Materials: Anthurium
Container: White vases

The anthurium flowers play a key role as the tips of the flames, and the red backlighting dramatically emphasizes the flames. This frank expression of fiery emotions embodies all our suppressed desires. The stunning impact of the arrangement is heightened by the white vases.

Note: In tone, the red lights and the anthurium should complement each other perfectly.

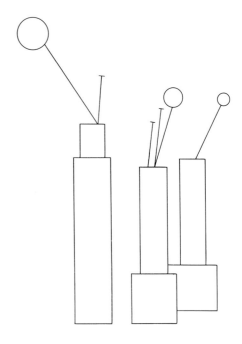

Theme: Merry Christmas

Materials: Monstera, Anthurium, Gomphus Carpus, Christmas ornaments, glass rod, cotton

Container: White glass vase

The colors of Christmas—white, red, and green—are much in evidence, conveying the season's warmth and cheer.

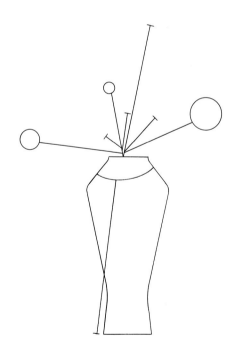

Theme: The Romance of Christmas
Materials: Basho leaf, Anthurium, Chinese Holly,
    Christmas ornaments, glass reindeer, cotton

The reindeer represents Christmas filled with romantic
dreams. Presents can be placed around this arrangement
just as around a Christmas tree.

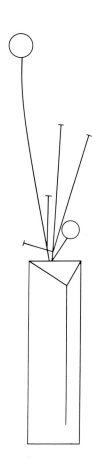

Travel

Theme: Victoria and Albert Museum
Materials: Gladiolus, Aspidistra, Balloon Vine
Container: Vase suitable for *nageire*

The aspidistra and the gladiolus flow downward with great dignity, and the balloon vine is entwined around the vase. The arrangement has a certain nobility, yet also a gentle delicacy. When Noriko Ohno was invited to attend the "Japan Festival 1991" in England as a representative of Japan, she gave demonstrations of ikebana and her creations were highly appreciated.

Note: Here it is necessary to use the *mizukiri* technique. Any buds on the tips of the gladiolus should be clipped off to strengthen the lines of the arrangement.

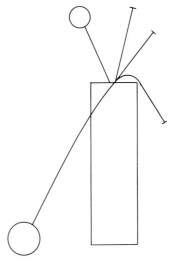

Theme: Romance
Materials: Rose, *Allium Schubertii* (dried)
Container: Large Roman urn dating from 200 A.D.

This arrangement is evocative of Roman times, when the urn was made, and this effect can be strengthened by placing it near a large window or next to marble.

Note: Use the *mizukiri* technique and dip the ends in wine or saké to prevent the growth of bacteria. Alternatively, you can burn the ends of the stems, as this will have the same effect.

ITALIAN
CERAMIC POT

Theme: An Image of Egypt: Pyramids and Camels
Materials: Lily, Heliconia, Pink Cushion
Container: Red, yellow, and white vases

This conjures up a striking, yet traditional image of Egypt, with camels striding majestically before the famous pyramids.

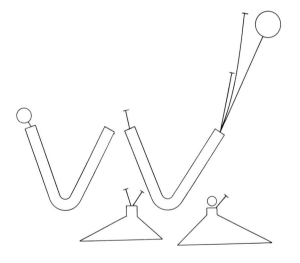

Theme: Prayers in the Mosque
Materials: Rose, Baby's Breath, Lilac
Container: Two vases

This arrangement was inspired by the sight of Moslems
kneeling in silent prayer in a mosque.

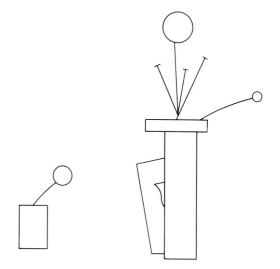

Theme: The Syrian Desert
Materials: Anthurium, fine plastic packing material
 from Italy
Container: Small ashtray

This is an evocation of the beauty of the desert and its hidden mystery.

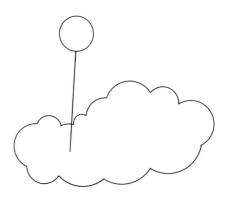

Theme: Mount Everest

Materials: Calla, Ornithogalum, Bear Grass, Philo-
dendron, Pampas, cotton

Container: Gray and white vases

The pampas frond placed vertically in the middle of the
arrangement conveys the height of this majestic mountain,
while the calla embodies its elegance and forbidding beauty.

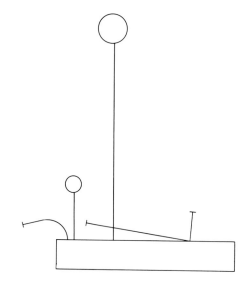

Theme: Beautiful Katmandu at the Foot of Mountains
Materials: Lily, Baby's Breath
Container: Vases made by a well-known Russian artist

This city's breathtaking beauty is represented by the two carefully selected vases. The sumptuous lilies and the frail beauty of the baby's breath express the energy flowing through this city.

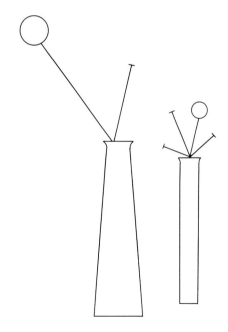

Theme: Cuba

Materials: Basho, Anthurium, Cuban handicrafts

Container: White vase

The robust cheerfulness of this Caribbean nation shines
out in this arrangement, with the tropical flowers express-
ing the charm of the people's lives.

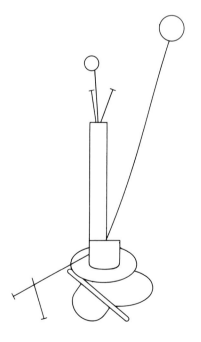

Theme: Venezuela

Materials: Anthurium, Venezuelan handicrafts

Amid the frenetic energy that bursts forth from this arrangement lies an intricate and entrancing beauty.

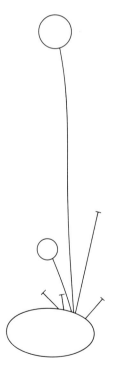

Theme: Dominica (*left*) and Nicaragua (*right*)
Materials: Garbera, Glory Lily, Chusan Palm
Container: Basket and two vases

Two vivacious and brilliant images of the peoples of these countries.

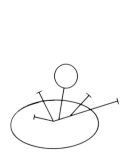
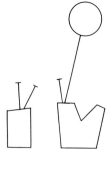

BASIC INSTRUCTIONS FOR
STUDENTS OF IKEBANA

BASIC METHODS AND STYLES

Chief branches

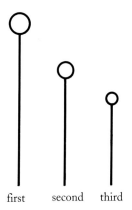

first   second   third

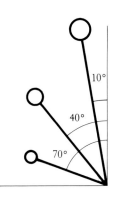

10°

40°

70°

Making ikebana arrangements involves certain basic methods and styles. The *moribana* ("piling flowers") method uses relatively shallow containers and *kenzan*, or needle point holders, to support the flowers and keep them in position, whereas the *nageire* ("tossed in") method uses tall containers and vases without *kenzan*. In both methods, the flowers are arranged into three main elements or branches, which I shall call branch groups, and the relative position of these results in four basic styles: upright, slanting, horizontal, and hanging. In addition, although in a natural arrangement the first and second branch groups always face left, they may be arranged to face right, which is called "a reverse arrangement."

The Three Branch Groups

In both the *moribana* and the *nageire* method, basic arrangements always contain three main compositional elements. Each of these branch groups may consist of a single flower, many flowers on the same stem, a leaf, or a tree branch with both flowers and leaves. The first branch group is the longest, the second is shorter, and the third is the shortest. In addition to these three, any number of subsidiary branches may be used to supplement one of the main branch groups.

The Length of the Branch Groups

The length of each main branch depends on the surroundings in which the arrangement is to be placed and on the materials to be used; it also must be in proportion with the width (A) and the depth (B) of the container or vase to be used. If you want to make a spectacularly large arrangement, the length of the first branch should be 2 x (A + B). In a medium-sized arrangement, the length of the first branch should be 1 1/2 x (A + B). In the case of a small arrangement, the length of the first branch should be (A + B).

The length of the remaining two branch groups is determined by the first main branch. The second branch should be 3/4 the length of the first, and the third should be 1/2 the length of the second. Subsidiary branches are usually shorter than the main branches.

The Four Basic Styles

Both *moribana* and *nageire* arrangements can be made in upright, slanting, horizontal, and hanging styles, which are achieved by varying the angles of the three main branch groups, depending on the materials used and the impression the arranger wants to convey. In any of the styles, *moribana* and *nageire* arrangements may use the same angles for the chief branches.

The **upright** style is characterized by a stationary, stable feeling. The accent is always on the first main branch, which seems to be reaching straight up to the heavens. Supporting branches in upright-style arrangements usually supplement one of the main branches, and in *moribana* arrangements they are used to cover the *kenzan*.

The **slanting** style is more rhythmical than the upright style. For the angled branch groups, be sure to insert the stems in the *kenzan* in an upright position first, and then gradually adjust them until they are in a sloping position.

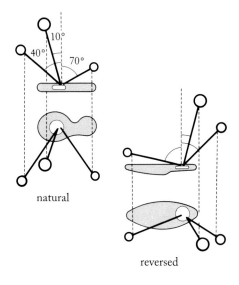

Upright Style

natural

reversed

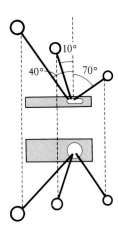

Slanting Style

Upright Style

1

2

3

Slanting Style

1

2

3

A **horizontal** style is best viewed from above, and floating flowers and glass containers are especially effective in this kind of arrangement. In this style, either use no *kenzan* at all, or keep it hidden with pebbles, sand, or subsidiary branches, taking care that no part of the *kenzan* is visible from any angle.

The **hanging** style is ideal for showing off the beautiful flowing lines of such materials as willow branches, eucalyptus, and vines. As the name implies, hanging-style arrangements may be hung on a wall—traditionally, hanging-style arrangements are hung in Japanese *tokonoma* alcoves—or placed on a shelf, where they can be viewed from above or below.

Horizontal Style

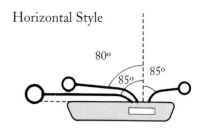

Hanging Style

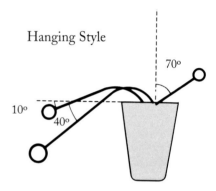

For an example of a hanging-style arrangement, please see p.39.

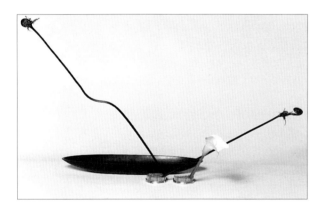

Variations

The possibilities for variations on these four basic styles are infinite, and the secret is to follow your own instincts and create in harmony with the flowers and materials. Some particular variations I have found to be successful are: the divided style, in which the chief branches are arranged in two separate *kenzan* placed apart in the container, which gives a sense of space; arrangements with floating flowers; and the duet style, where baby's breath or another material is placed near each of the main branches to form a sort of duet with it. The *moribana* and *nageire* arrangements can also be displayed together in a combination of containers, and sometimes the containers themselves will suggest new variations—for example, when they have more than one opening. The Morimono style that combines flowers and fruits is another possibility. As your joy in creating arrangements increases and your understanding of the flowers deepens, you will be able to conceive of endless variations of your own.

Container with two openings

Floating Flowers

In any floating flower composition, the water itself should be "arranged" with as much care as the flowers. If possible, avoid using a *kenzan* at all, but if you have to use one, choose the smallest one possible and hide it well with pebbles or other materials. Glassware or natural materials such as seashells work wonderfully as containers. Position the arrangement so that it can be viewed from above.

Floating flower arrangement

UTENSILS

Pruning Shears

At the hardware store, ask for "*warabite*" shears, and be sure to try out several pairs in order to find one that fits your hand best. Remember that if the shears are too stiff or too loose, they will be difficult to use. At first they may seem a little awkward, but with practice you will soon get used to them. From time to time rub some oil on your shears to keep them working smoothly.

Warabite shears

Kenzan (Needle Point Holders)

The most common *kenzan* are round or crescent-shaped, and they may be used either separately or in combination. If your arrangement involves large flowers or leaves, rectangular *kenzan* are preferable are they are more stable. Extremely small *kenzan* are now common for arrangements in glassware containers and very small vessels. If your *kenzan* is not as steady as you wish, place small pebbles on top of it and around it. When the container is of silver, place silver foil under the *kenzan* to protect the metal. If *kenzan* are not available, use a few stones the size of your fist or smaller to support the flowers.

Kenzan

Water Spray (Pump)

Your arrangements can be rendered much more vivid and alive if you spray them with water—especially in hot, sultry summer weather. The bugle-shaped head section of this water spray can be reversed to convert it into a water pump to force water into the stems of such aquatic plants as lotuses, water lilies, and candocks.

Water spray

Saws

Although a pair of pruning shears will be adequate in most cases, a small saw (or ax) is convenient for cutting tougher branches.

Saws

Wire

Wire can be used to tie materials together, and a rough ball of it is an excellent substitute for a *kenzan*, especially in small containers such as glasses.

Needle-Repairer

Kenzan needles are liable to bend, so this device is useful for straightening the needles easily.

Needle-repairer

Water-Change Pump

In order to change the water in the containers, use a siphon-type rubber pump.

Water-change pump

Pebbles and Sand (Black and White)

If you cover the *kenzan* with small pebbles you can make your arrangements very natural and realistic. For an interesting contrast, use white pebbles in black containers, and black pebbles in white containers. Occasionally, sand is also a convenient alternative.

Preservation Liquids (Chemicals)

In order to prevent decay, certain chemicals—such as alcohol, acetic acid, and peppermint oil—may be applied to the cut stems of materials. Salt is also very effective in preventing decay.

Pebbles and other accessories

MATERIALS

Flowers and Branches

Almost all ikebana arrangements consist of combinations of flowers, branches, and leaves, but any material that fits your mental image and matches the intended setting may also be used. Generally, in a single arrangement you should combine two or more types of plants. However, you can also create beautiful effects with flowers of a single species, such as camellias, daffodils, cherry boughs, irises, sweet flags, clematis, cosmos, or roses of one color. Select forms and colors that harmonize. Your own sense of beauty will inspire you when blending and contrasting shapes, colors, and lines.

Dried Materials

Many variations of dried materials are commercially available, but your autumn and winter arrangements will acquire a distinctive personality if you incorporate materials you prepare yourself. Go into the woods and fields and gather berries and grasses that appeal to you, bring them home, dry them, and use them in your arrangements, either alone or in combination with other materials. Arrangements of dried materials have a beauty and elegance appreciated by people all over the world.

Other Natural Materials

There are countless combinations of vegetables, vines, fruits, roots, driftwood, dead branches, gourds, pumpkins, berries, and other natural materials of all shapes and colors that can make appealing arrangements and may be used as table centerpieces.

Artificial Materials

In modern arrangements, ikebana artists are increasingly incorporating artificial materials together with natural materials. This is particularly true for some settings such as show windows or exhibitions, when the materials have to last longer than natural flowers and branches. Plastics, steel wire, and glass are all effective, but it takes practice to make arrangements with artificial materials as emotionally satisfying as those with natural materials. For long-lasting displays, first try dried, bleached, or otherwise processed natural materials.

Water

If your flower arrangement can achieve a sense of coolness, it can be wonderfully refreshing. In such arrangements, try using as little of the materials as possible, and leave at least two-thirds of the water surface free of flowers. Frequent changes of water in the container will preserve flowers longer and keep the water looking fresh and clean. In hot weather, try putting some ice cubes into the water. When you spray water onto the leaves, take care not to wet the flowers.

CONTAINERS

A question I am often asked is: What are most beautiful containers? However, it is a question I cannot answer satisfactorily. This is because, in the art of flower arrangement, containers exist not in isolation but only in combination with the flowers and other materials. Always give full consideration to the flowers you are going to use when selecting the container so that together they will harmonize perfectly as regards color, shape, and other respects. Containers should also complement the surroundings in which the arrangements are to be placed.

Containers may be divided into two major categories—those created intentionally as vases for flower arrangements and those borrowed for this purpose. You can find potential containers everywhere—fruit baskets, straw hats, ordinary bottles, jugs, and cut glass, just to mention a few. Sections of bamboo can also make excellent containers.

The safest colors for containers are black and white. Remember that the simplest shapes will harmonize with almost every kind of materials. Avoid containers that have elaborate designs as these are liable to clash with the images you are trying to create with the flowers. Try to find potential flower containers around you and develop your sense of beauty by using them in as many different ways as possible. Folk-art wares that were made for a practical purpose can also make interesting vehicles for your arrangements. With these and other objects, you can create unexpectedly beautiful arrangements that would be unsuitable in more usual flower containers.

Always remember that successful arrangements are the result of the harmonious combination of materials, containers, and your own lifestyle and environment.

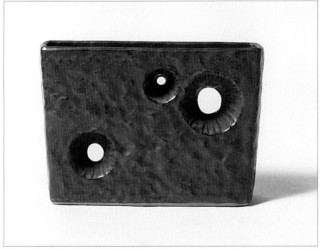

TRIMMING TECHNIQUES

Skill with Scissors

Slip the top handle of the scissors over your thumb, and let it rest well down, at the base of your thumb. The bottom handle should rest in the joints of the other four fingers. The cutting action comes from firmly and steadily closing your entire hand, not your finger-tips alone. Some people insert only their index finger in the handle to cut, but this only reduces the strength you are applying. The quickest way to attain a good cutting technique is to imagine that the scissors are hanging on your thumb and let the rest of your hand do the work.

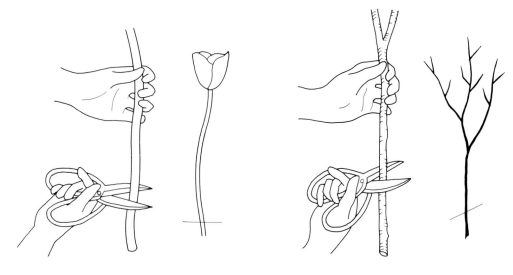

Right-angle cut   Diagonal cut

Cut fleshy stems at right angles when using a *kenzan*.

Cut branches on an angle to increase water intake.

Flowers

Although in a natural setting a haphazard profusion of flowers can be delightful, for ikebana arrangements we must select just those flowers that create the mood or achieve the effect we want. First, clip away all withered or crushed blossoms; next, carefully examine the material, and trim away everything but the flowers you are sure will contribute to the effect you desire.

If you are going to use a *kenzan*, you should cut the stems of fleshy plants at right angles, for a diagonal cut will result in a fragile end that may split on the needles. However, if your container is a deep vase which does not require a *kenzan*, cutting stems on the diagonal will increase the exposed area and the stem's intake of water.

Always give stems and stalks a clean cut; avoid chopping them raggedly.

Branches

Trimming is a way to abbreviate and improve the natural look of branches. When trimming, do not be timid but clip away boldly—your arrangements are sure to be much livelier if you do so. Try to cut branches only where they fork, because otherwise you will leave unsightly scars. If you have to cut away a large leaf or cut a branch midway and leave a scar as a result, disguise this by applying a little India ink.

Leaves

Cut leaves to emphasize particular strong points in line and color. Bear in mind the beauty of the plant's characteristics and study the branch carefully when selecting the leaves to remove. Be sure that only the leaves that will play a vital part in your arrangement will remain. In ikebana there is no room for non-essentials.

Leaves can be manipulated in various ways to give your arrangements a sense of movement. Roll the tips of wide leaves with your fingers to achieve a gentle curl, and pass the tops of slender leaves through a slit in the center vein to make an interesting ribbon-like effect.

 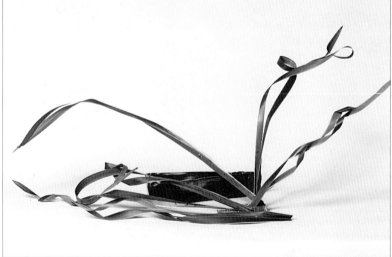

BENDING MATERIALS

Basic Method

Keep your elbows close to your body and apply pressure with your thumbs at the point you want to bend. If the material is a fleshy, grasslike plant, crush it lightly beforehand at the point you want to bend. When done gently, this will not damage the tough, water-transporting fibers of even the most delicate plants.

Slitting and Bending

Some thick woody stalks and branches offer so much resistance that it is difficult to bend them using the above basic method. Slitting at the point you want to bend will enable you to shape the branch properly. However, be warned that careless use of the knife will weaken stalks and branches so that they break easily.

Wedging and Bending

On branches too tough even for the above slitting method, make a cut on the outside with a saw. The depth of the cut will depend upon the texture of the wood, but in most cases a cut about two-thirds the diameter of the branch will suffice. Find another branch of about the same thickness as the one you are working with, and, using your saw, cut from it a V-shaped wedge thick enough to achieve the desired bend and deep enough to fill the slit in the first branch.

FIXING MATERIALS IN VASES

Since *nageire* arrangements are made without a *kenzan*, many techniques have been developed to help the materials stand in their vases in attractive and natural ways.

Slitting the Stalk
For most deep jar- and bottle-shaped vases, cut small pieces of branch in lengths that will fit firmly either horizontally or diagonally across the inside of the vase. Cut slits in the bottoms of the stems of the floral materials and fit them on the brace in the vase.

No Braces
Place one stalk in the vase so that it is stable and prop all the other flowers against it.

Single-Flower Prop
Fix a single flower in place by propping it against the side of a vase.

straight   diagonal

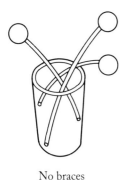

No braces

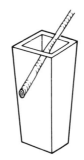

Single-flower prop

Fork prop

Fork Prop

Cut off a short length of stalk, cut slits in it and in the bottom of the material, fit the two together, and put them into the vase.

Cross Brace

To space the flowers more widely, make a cross by tying short sections of stalk together. Slip the cross into the vase, and arrange the materials around it.

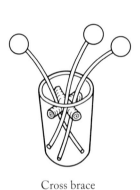

Cross brace

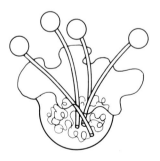

Wire holder

Wire Holder

If the shape or material of the vase makes a *kenzan* or stick braces look unsightly or impractical, make up a ball of fine wire, place it in the bottom of the vase, and put the materials in it.

Applications

To arrange branches horizontally in tall containers, use the slit-stalk method, with a supporting branch slightly longer than the vase.

Place the branches in the vase. Be sure to hide the supporting branch carefully with stalks of leaves or flowers.

Hollow stems like this amaryllis require a short branch to support them when a *kenzan* is used.

Cut the supporting stalk slightly longer than the stem of the amaryllis, position it in the *kenzan*, and slip the amaryllis over the stalk.

METHODS TO PRESERVE FLOWERS

The *Mizukiri* Cutting Method
Place the stems of the materials in a bucket or deep bowl filled with fresh water. With your shears under the water, cut one-inch pieces from the stalks until the materials are the length you want for your arrangement. After cutting, leave the materials in the water for about ten minutes because the water pressure promotes water intake.

Cutting under water (*mizukiri*)

Flowers Direct from the Garden
Always try to cut flowers from your garden either early in the morning or after sunset. Fill a container with water and take it with you so that you can immediately cut your flowers under water and let them stand in it for a good drink. Be especially sure to do this with flowers such as morning glories and hydrangeas. Sprinkle a pinch of salt around camellia stamens, and spray the blossom with a fine mist. The salt will cause the pollen to rise and prevent the flower from shedding its petals. To prevent camellia petals falling off, insert a toothpick or pin at the base of the flower.

Flowers Needing Extra Water

Materials that have been out of water for a long time, such as flowers gathered on a trip to the country, should be given a chance to take in water before they are cut. Dip the materials in cold water, wrap them in newspaper, moisten the paper, and lay the flowers on their sides for about thirty minutes in a place sheltered from wind and sunlight.

Charring

Wrap flowers in paper and quickly char the cut ends of the stems over a gas flame, an alcohol lamp, or a candle. Then immediately dip the ends in cold water. Carbonizing the ends stimulates the plant and prevents the growth of bacteria.

Hot-Water Treatment

Wrap the blossoms and upper parts of the materials in paper, as in the charring method above, and dip the cut ends in hot water. This method is effective for tender, soft materials that would be damaged by the charring method.

Cutting and Crushing

Making horizontal and vertical cuts in the ends of materials or crushing the ends with scissors will improve their ability to take in water.

Applying Chemicals

After cutting the materials in water, rub the cut ends of the stems with chemicals such as salt, baking soda, burnt alum, and so on. Alternatively, you can dissolve these chemicals in the water in the flower vase. This method is effective for all kinds of plants. Salt is especially effective for plants such as Chinese bellflowers and garbella.

Treatment with Chemicals

This method is used to sterilize flowers. After cutting the materials, place them in diluted alcohol, acetic acid, peppermint oil, or ammonia for ten to twenty minutes. Be careful not to make the solution too strong or the plants will wither. A couple of drops of apple vinegar in the water in the vase is also very effective. Acetic acid is good for plants such as pampas grass and millet, while alcohol is best for wisteria and other vines.

Pumping Water

To give lotuses and water lilies the extra water they require, prepare a solution of tobacco water by wrapping cigarette ends in cloth and soaking them in water, or a tea solution by boiling tea until it is quite strong. Using your water pump, fill the stalk of the leaves and the blossoms with either one of these solutions, and seal the cut end with alum. This will help fresh and healthy materials last longer.

Water pumping

A LIFE WITH FLOWERS

Noriko Ohno was born in 1920 and began her studies of formal ikebana in 1937, after graduating from high school. She studied classical and formal arrangements with the Ikenobo Ryuseiha school and learned the basics of modern *moribana* and *nageire* with the Sogetsu school. Her dream of multinational and multicultural ikebana began to take form while she was holding classes in flower arrangement for non-Japanese students at the American Club in Tokyo. Beginning with her work as a cultural envoy in 1954, she soon became very active on the international scene, traveling around the world to give demonstrations and exhibitions of ikebana at the invitation of public and private organizations. The following chronology is a record of her major achievements over a half century of commitment to the world of ikebana.

1954–55: Selected to participate in São Paulo's 400th anniversary celebrations as a cultural envoy; thereafter spent one year giving floral demonstrations in cities throughout North and South America, Europe, the Middle East, and Southeast Asia ; her ikebana exhibition organized at the invitation of the French government was the first of its kind to be held in Paris. Upon her return to Japan in April 1955, she founded the Kokusai Ikebana Association.

1958: Represented the Japanese government at the Brussels World's Fair.

1961: Participated in the International Modern Design Exhibition in Switzerland.

1963: Gave demonstrations at the Musée Guimet in France and in many European countries; gave demonstrations at Hawaii's East-West Center; donated a glass art relief, "Flowers Are Living," to São Paulo's Japan Culture Center; interviewed celebrities around the world for *Josei Jishin* magazine, creating ikebana arrangements for each one.

1964: Inaugurated the Monthly Charity Show. In the past twenty-six years, one hundred and fifty embassies have sponsored these shows.

1966: Gave demonstrations at the Musée Guimet in Paris, the Instituto Italiano in Rome, and the Cologne Japan Culture Center in West Germany.

1967: Interviewed successful women around the world for the *Fujin Koron* magazine, presenting each one with an ikebana portrait.

1968: Was honorary guest of the government of Yugoslavia; served as judge at the first Monte Carlo Flora Competition; held a charity show at Tokyo's Kabukiza theater.

1973: Constructed the Kokusai Ikebana Gakuin bulding, the "Castle of Flowers," in the Aoyama district of Tokyo.

1974: Gave ikebana demonstrations in Switzerland at the invitation of the Association Suisse–Japon.

1975: Visited Brazil under the sponsorship of the Japan Foundation and there received the Brazilian government's Cultural Medal; gave demonstrations in Paraguay, Peru, and the United States (Pasadena).

1977: Dedicated an ikebana arrangement to the Japan Red Cross on the opening of its new building; visited Czechoslovakia and Hungary under the sponsorship of the Japan Foundation; presented Malaysia's prime minister with a floral arrangement to celebrate his visit to Japan.

1978: Participated in a charity show for the Chinese Women's Association in Singapore; gave demonstrations at the opening of East Germany's Trade Center.

1979: Gave demonstrations throughout Italy; was awarded the Gold Medal of Friendship.

1980: Gave demonstrations in Tunisia, Belgium, and France.

1981: Visited Kokusai Ikebana chapters in Malaysia, Singapore, and Taipei; attended Bulgaria's 1300th anniversary celebrations; gave demonstrations at the EC Hall in Belgium for its foreign ministry.

1982: Gave her 1000th demonstration abroad.

1983: Gave demonstrations in Paris, Denmark, and the Netherlands; was awarded a Gold Medal by Singapore's Red Cross.

1984: Held a floral exhibition in Majorca, Spain; attended the Japan–U.S.S.R. Roundtable Conference; gave demonstrations in Moscow, Tallinn, and Leningrad.

1985: Gave demonstrations in Malaysia, Singapore, and Taipei; gave demonstrations throughout Brazil, sponsored by the Japan Foundation; received the Grand Cross cultural medal from the Brazilian government.

1986: Gave demonstrations in Singapore, Malta, Assisi (25th anniversary of the World Wildlife Fund), Belgium, Poland, Bulgaria, and Austria.

1987: Visited Malaysia and Taipei; attended Japan Week in New Zealand; gave demonstrations in Australia.

1988: Attended the Singapore Community Chest Show; gave demonstrations in Taiwan, in Malaysia, and at Australia's Bicentennial celebrations; attended the Japan–U.S.S.R. Roundtable Conference; gave demonstrations in Moscow and Tallinn.

1989: Gave demonstrations in the Baltic states; attended Belgium's Europalia Japan 1989 as a cultural envoy; presented Queen Fabiola of Belgium with an ikebana arrangement; gave demonstrations in Paris and Luxembourg.

1990: Visited Singapore, Hong Kong, and Taiwan; held an exhibition at the Osaka International Garden and Greenery Exposition; held the 35th Anniversary Exhibition of Kokusai Ikebana at the Printemps department store in Ginza in Tokyo.

1991: Was made an honorary citizen of the city of São Paulo and given the key of the state of São Paulo; gave demonstrations at the Victoria and Albert Museum during the Japan Festival 1991 in London.

1992: Held the "Song of Flower" exhibition in Singapore and in nations of the South Pacific; received a citation from the foreign minister of Japan; visited England, Bulgaria, and Morocco.

1994: Visited Latin American countries, including Nicaragua, Venezuela, Cuba, and Dominica; was awarded the National Culture Medal by Cuba's minister of culture.